SO-AFR-338

Psychoanalytic Thought for Youth

ABOUT DREAMS

By Suzanne T. Saldarini

Illustrated by Lou Simeone

Copyright © 2013 by Suzanne T. Saldarini

All rights reserved.

For permissions to reproduce more than 300 words of this publication, email to ORIPressEditor@Gmail.com or write to ORI Academic Press Editor @ 7515 187th St, Fresh Meadows, NY 11366.

Printed in the United States of America on acid free paper.

Library of Congress Control Number: 2013920645

ISBN-13: 978-0-9848700-4-2

ISBN-13: 978-0-9848700-6-6 (color)

eISBN-13: 978-0-9848700-5-9

Illustrations - by Lou Simeone @ www.lousimeone.com.

mindmendmedia
piecing it together

Book design and editing - by MindMendMedia, Inc. @ www.MindMendMedia.com

Dedication

to

Kristen and Ronnie

Joe, Johnathan

Cassie, Ozzie

and

Thomas Kai

PUBLISHER'S PREFACE

ORI Academic Press is proud to present you with the first book in the *Psychoanalytic Thought for Youth* series. This new series aims to make the internal world more accessible to the younger generation, helping parents and teachers navigate conversations about such difficult topics as dream-work, emotions, behaviors, and - of course - understanding oneself and others.

ORI Academic Press Staff

New York, 2013

AUTHOR'S PREFACE

About Dreams is an invitation. I hope readers aged eight to thirteen - and the adults who care for them - will use this story to explore the mysteries dreams (especially scary ones) present to all of us.

The story begins with Truman, an ordinary boy who has an extraordinarily frightening dream. We learn about events in his life and then pause to meet the most famous dream-reader of all - Sigmund Freud. Dr. Freud, a distinguished nineteenth century neurologist, recognized dreams as worthy of careful study. He approached them with close observation, developed a theory to explain their origins, content, meaning and function and used his discoveries to form a psychology which still supports research and treatment

Freud's ideas and his way of working provide special ways to think about Truman's dream and any others we might meet. I hope readers will test what they've learned on our story's second dream, this time a silly one dreamed by an adult. By the way, the people in this story are made-up, but the dreams are real.

About Dreams can be enjoyed alone, read aloud, or even used in school. Health, Guidance, Science or Writing teachers might find many ways to add dream study to class work.

If readers have even some of the fun reading that I've had writing this little book will be a real success. I'll end my too-long preface here with grateful acknowledgements: thanks to Inna Rozentsvit for boldly supporting this quirky project and to Ron Saldarini for lovingly supporting its quirky author.

Suzanne Saldarini

Mahwah NJ, 2013

INTRODUCTION

In the 1940's, an exciting program called *The Shadow* opened this way: a deep male voice, dripping radio drama, intoned, "Who knows what evil lurks in the hearts of men?" *"The Shadow* knows!" Resonating laughter follows. Scary shows like **The Shadow** were off limits to my brother and I but somehow I managed to borrow that laughter, add heavy approaching footsteps, and create a nightmare so terrifying it woke me screaming every night for a year. I was four. My exhausted parents were counseled against worry: "She'll grow out of it," – "it's the ear infections" (the dream included covering my ears with my hands), and "she has a calcium deficiency." I was made to drink an odious concoction of water and white powder each night before bed, "so you won't have bad dreams."

The Shadow disappeared with my fifth birthday. He was replaced with years of other dreams, but, fortunately with few like him. His nightly visits however, left me with a lingering respect for the world of dreams. I chose psychology at school, read Freud, and finally studied psychoanalysis. My interest in dreams grew into something like a quest. *About Dreams* came from that search.

Dreamers young and old know that dreams fill wishes. A coveted possession, a reunion with an old friend, even a wish to sleep a bit longer can all be arranged by our sleeping minds. Frightening dreams, however, are at odds with wish-filling. Where do such scary images come from? Will these bad things really happen? Why dream anyway? Freud and today's dream researchers find special challenges in these mysteries. Still, applying psychoanalytic method, that is, observing connections between events, decisions, wishes and feelings – especially those denied expression – reveals useful information about these disturbing communications. When we help dreamers, both adults and children, use problem solving skills in response to even the most uncomfortable of dreams, we affirm the importance of internal, private, and perhaps secret emotional life. Solving personal mysteries leads the way to confidence and competence.

PART ONE: TRUMAN'S DREAM

A boy named Truman had a terrible and frightening dream. Here it is:

Truman and his family are all together driving in their car. Suddenly there is a terrible storm. Thunder crashes and lightning flashes. Rain blows against the windshield. The car is pushed around by great gusts of wind. Truman becomes more and more frightened. His father grips the wheel and tries to hold the car on the highway but he can't do it! The car is torn from the road. It turns and twists in the air, rising higher and higher. It's turned upside down and the doors fly open. Everyone falls out of their seat-belts. They spin downward. Truman watches helplessly – he's terrified. He looks down and sees each member of his family hit the ground. They lie flat and still. Are they dead or alive? Truman is falling fast and sees the ground racing up to meet him. His heart is beating very fast;

he's spinning out of control. "It's over!" he yells, and wakes up feeling very scared.

Thursday, the day before the dream, Truman came home from school as usual. "Better finish up that science project," said his Mom, "Tomorrow we're going to Aunt Serena's for the weekend."

"What?" exclaimed Truman, "Who says? I don't want to go there for the whole week-end!"

"It's all set," said his mother, "we're going. First chance we've had for weeks."

"No one told me," complained Truman, "and I don't want to go."

Truman was really angry. This was the first weekend without soccer since the start of the season. Saturday, with no practice and no game, he'd lie on the couch all day and watch cartoons. And eat Fruit Loops. He'd finish his science project on Sunday. It was on weather – no big deal. Now all that was spoiled.

Truman hated the long drive to Aunt Serena's. Belted into the back seat forever. His baby sister threw chewed-up Gold Fish all over the place and his brother always got to pick the video. Besides, his cousins, Anna, Hanna, and Rosemarie (Aunt Serena's triplet girls) always made fun of his name and he wasn't allowed to do anything back. Serena raised poodles, and the puppies always peed on Truman when he tried to play with them. Truman also hated the way his mother got all sing-songy over her sister. So what if she raised prize-winning poodles and had triplets and ran a pharmaceutical company? Who cares? Truman didn't. "That Serena," his mother would say, "She does so much! She just blows me away!"

Truman felt angry all over again. He really wished he didn't have to go. Still, he pushed those feelings away. He'd never convince his parents to stay home. He sighed. He went downstairs and banged on his drums. "I'm practicing," he yelled, "if anyone cares!" After awhile Truman came back upstairs. His mother smiled at him. "Storm over?" she asked.

"Yeah," grumbled Truman, "It's over."

***

Dreams are mysteries and can't always be solved. Still, here's a list of facts to help us play detective with Truman's dream.

1. Truman was very angry. He was being forced to do something he didn't want to do. His own plans were spoiled and no one seemed to care.

2. Truman also felt helpless and stuck. He pushed his anger and other uncomfortable feelings away.

3. On the night of the dream Truman went to sleep with a lot on his mind. We know this included:

a) A wish that he didn't have to travel to Aunt Serena's.

b) Anger and other uncomfortable feelings held down

c) A conversation with his mother.

d) Many stored-up facts about weather.

4. With his conscious mind asleep, his unconscious took charge (more about these two parts of our mind later). It invented a terrible storm which

filled Truman's wish – and it disguised that wish. No one can be blamed for bad weather.

5. Truman's unconscious mind went too far. When the stormy dream started killing people – and even threatened to kill Truman – it scared the conscious part of his mind awake and killed the dream.

6. In Truman's dream bad things happened to people he loved; does that mean he wished for those things to happen? The dream filled a wish, but the way the wish was filled did not please Truman.

Part Two explains how all this works.

PART TWO: TWO MINDS

Your mind – and everyone else's – is like an iceberg. It has two parts: conscious and unconscious. The conscious part is the piece sticking up out of the water; it's easily seen. The unconscious part is much bigger. It's submerged, huge and invisible. These two pieces make up two kinds of mental activity or systems.

The conscious system is the one we all know best. This part gives us words for what we see, hear, feel and think. It remembers, pays attention, solves problems and knows right from wrong. It makes decisions, is in charge of when and how we move, and lets us know our body feelings. It imagines, and invents, and learns new things all the time. It also lets us know who we are – the "I" we speak, think, feel and know about. The conscious mind tells us about the world around us and what to think about that world. It also tells us about our private – inside – world.

Well, at least something about that private inside world. The unconscious, the biggest part of the mind (remember the ice-berg), is private and mostly hidden – even from ourselves. It is huge and full of energy. It stores everything we experience. Some of this is useful – like all the "how-to's" we've learned and forgotten (e.g. how to talk, walk, separate familiar from strange, etc.). Some is useless – like the color T-shirt your friend wore on Tuesday. Some of this stuff gets used all the time – some may never be used again. Out-law thoughts and ideas and wishes – thoughts the conscious mind doesn't want to have or doesn't like to have or believes it shouldn't have – are stored (imprisoned, actually) in the unconscious.

The conscious mind is in charge of this great messy mass. It's also in charge of connections with the outside world (talking, walking, and deciding). The unconscious mind cares only about what it wants and feels; it cares nothing about anything involved in actually filling wants or taking care of feelings.

The unconscious mind is hard to know –
because it's unconscious! But here's a way to think
about it. It reacts only to what feels good or bad; it
avoids bad feelings and seeks good ones. It doesn't
know or care about common sense, right or wrong,
safe or dangerous. It's a lot like a toddler: sometimes
content, sometimes angry, always demanding and
caring only about its own wishes. It doesn't really
think; instead, it stores up picture-memories of what
was pleasing or displeasing. These picture memories
are old and new and get all mixed up together.

PART THREE: DR. FREUD

More than 100 years ago, Dr. Sigmund Freud, an Austrian doctor who studied the brain, discovered that dreams could be used to look into the hidden, submerged, unconscious part of ourselves. When his patients told him about their pains and worries, he noticed that they often talked about dreams. When they talked more – speaking about dreams in a very free way (Dr. Freud listened carefully and did not criticize or argue with his patients' ideas), more thoughts and memories came up. Often, these were thoughts patients hadn't seen before, or forgotten, or didn't even know they had (thought they shouldn't have), or didn't want to have.

The conscious part of their thinking had left them unsaid. Dr. Freud observed that when patients spoke about these ideas and expressed feelings, they felt better and thought more clearly. Encouraging patients to speak freely about memories, thoughts and ideas, and understanding their feelings became Dr. Freud's best way of helping people. He also formed many useful hypotheses (careful guesses) about how the mind works. For example, he worked out the ideas about the two parts of the mind described in Part Two.

Dr. Freud gave special attention to dreams – his own and others. He observed and studied them carefully. He started out with simple facts that we all know, like dreams happen only when we're sleeping. He went on to theorize that only the conscious mind sleeps. The unconscious, like a hyper-active toddler, never sleeps. It keeps up a constant demand to have its wishes filled. Without the conscious mind awake to scold or soothe it, its wishes sneak out in the form of dreams (more about this later).

You know that when scientists study things they organize what they find. For example, biologists classify (sort) animals into groups, like mammals, reptiles and fishes. The animals' characteristics – perhaps fur, scales, or feathers – make up the types. Sorting organizes facts and helps us to learn more. As

Dr. Freud's observations about dreams grew he sorted them. His list is too long for us but we'll look at three of the most common kinds. This includes the scary kinds, even though they are the hardest to understand and explain.

1) Dreams That Fill Wishes

These are fun dreams and are easy to understand. Maybe you've always wanted to drive a race-car. In your sleep – there you are, speeding around the track. For as long as the dream lasts your unconscious makes your wish a fact. It feels like you are really on the track and really driving. For the unconscious, wishes and reality are the same thing.

Sometimes the unconscious tries to fill a physical need (a particular kind of wish) with a dream. If you go to bed hungry you might dream of your favorite food. Of course, dreaming of a Big Mac will not fill your empty stomach, so eventually the dream's way of filling your wish fails and the still-hungry feeling wakes you up. Still, the unconscious and conscious worked together here; the unconscious cooked up a Big Mac and tried to let you sleep a little longer.

Dr. Freud learned that all dreams start with wishes. This is hard to believe because dreams are so often unpleasant; many show scary, terrible things we would never want to happen. Sometimes people dream someone they love is hurt or killed. No one would wish for that! In fact, we usually push away even a hint of such thoughts. We want to keep painful ideas out of our minds and never know anything about them. Figuring out the second kind of dream - frightening, bad ones - is difficult, but, like solving a mystery, it can be done.

2) <u>Scary Dreams</u>:

<u>Someone Loved is Hurt or Killed</u>

In the Big Mac dream two wishes – one to eat and one to stay asleep – were filled. But sometimes the two parts of the mind don't cooperate so well. When the unconscious has an idea or memory the conscious doesn't want, it fights against knowing it. The unconscious doesn't give up; instead it hides the idea in something else, sneaking it by in a disguise. The fight against unwanted ideas continues even when we sleep, but, in sleep, the conscious mind is less watchful. It is not bothered by silly, nonsensical thoughts and doesn't see that they are dangerous ideas camouflaged. This is one of the main reasons dreams have so many strange images.

One more fact about sleep and dreams is very important: the unconscious mind has no power to make us walk or move around; only the conscious mind can do that. So, no matter what wild or bad or nutty ideas the unconscious comes up with, nothing bad can happen.

3) Crazy Nonsense Dreams

Some dreams don't wake us up at all. They also don't tell much of a story, have few feelings in them, and lots of impossibly mixed up pictures and ideas. They are very hard to figure out. Dr. Freud discovered that in these dreams, like Truman's storm dream, the wish is one the dreamer doesn't (consciously) like, and so it is disguised. A secret, even from the dreamer.

Aunt Serena had such a dream:

Aunt Serena is at an important meeting. She sits in an auditorium filled with people. There is an enormous stage at the front. Important people from the pharmaceutical industry are seated on the stage; they are brightly lighted. Aunt Serena recognizes one person, Dr. X. He is a very important man that everyone admires and respects. His long legs are neatly crossed in front of him and his hands rest in a dignified way on the arms of his big chair. He wears a serious, thoughtful and intelligent expression of his face – and nothing else. Dr. X. is completely naked! Well, almost completely – he wears a pair of Jockey shorts on his head!

If you wanted to help Aunt Serena understand her dream, what questions would you ask? How would you listen? Crazy Nonsense dreams may seem unimportant, but they may be the most important of all. That's because they let us sleep. Dr. Freud learned that dreams' usefulness comes with their power to protect our sleeping minds.

AFTERWORD:
AN INVITATION FOR
TEACHERS

Use *About Dreams* to bring dream-study to your class-
room. Dreams arouse curiosity, engage observation,
and stir empathy. Best of all, including dreams for
work at school shows children our respect for internal
life; feelings, fears, memories and wishes all matter!
Go to (http://orinyc.org/About-Dreams-Saldarini.html)
and download practical steps and an annotated
bibliography prepared to make dream-work accessible
to you and your students.

CPSIA information can be obtained at www.ICGtesting.com
Printed in the USA
BVIW12n1218110115
382622BV00001B/1